A Christmas box

Chris S. Stephens

pont
library

Contents

Introduction: Christmas Boxes	3
Christmas Cards	4
Why the Robin's Breast is Red	6
The Nativity	8
Plygain	10
Christmas Recipes	11
Father Christmas and Christmas presents	12
Christmas Books	14
Games and Parties	15
Evergreens	16
Heron, Cat and Bramble: a folk tale	18
The Angel	19
Pantomimes	20
The Wren	22
Wassailing	24
A Gower Wassail Song	26
Calennig	27
Mari Lwyd	28
New Year Traditions	30
Acknowledgements	32

Christmas Boxes

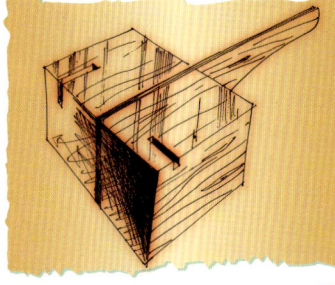

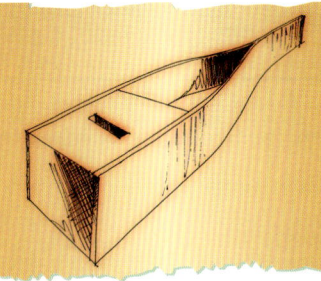

A Christmas Box is traditionally a gift of money given to servants, tradesmen or trainees, to thank them for a year's hard work. Perhaps your parents or your grandparents will remember a time when the postman, the newspaper boy, the egg lady, even the bin men received a folded envelope containing their Christmas 'box'.

The first Christmas boxes, from the Middle Ages, were either wooden boxes placed in churches, or pottery boxes carried around by apprentices. These were the young people who were learning a trade, like office clerks, carpenters and weavers.

Churchgoers put money, or alms, in the boxes, which were opened once a year on December 26th and shared amongst the poor. This is where the name Boxing Day comes from. The young workers would smash the pottery boxes when they were full, and use the money to pay for a grand feast – of much better food than they could usually afford.

This book is in itself a Christmas Box, containing something for everyone to share – poems, legends, information, pictures and photographs, all from Wales. Some are from the present, some from the past, rather like the contents of a Christmas decorations box, taken down from the loft or from the top of the wardrobe early in December. It is full of memories of the past, and the promise of many exciting Christmases to come.

Turn the page,
open the Christmas Box,
and enjoy yourself!

Christmas Cards

HARK THE HERALD ANGELS SING!

Christmas cards, and the Christmas postbox in the school corridor, are often the first signs of Christmas. Cards are a good way of keeping in touch with people whom we don't see often. In fact the first Christmas card was designed by John Callcott Horsley for his friend Henry Cole who didn't have enough time to write proper letters to everyone he knew at Christmas time in 1843. He began a tradition which was helped by Roland Hill's penny post, and the halfpenny post, although it now costs much more – even for a second class stamp!

Here are a selection of Christmas cards from the last 150 years; many of them have particular links with Wales.

This 1928 'Hearty Greeting' card travelled from Siberia to Carmarthen. The franking suggests it was sent from a sailor on one of King George V's ships.

Cards and postcards often have the name of the town or village from which they were sent – even if, like the one from Moylegrove, they were printed in Germany!

Although Christmas cards often feature traditional scenes, with robins, snowed-up mailcoaches and village churches with stained-glass windows, cartoon cards and pictures of children have always been popular too.

Home-made Christmas cards, like this one from the Jones family, sent in 1948, have a special charm, and become treasured possessions. Making a card – and often a calendar as well – have become a highlight of Christmas preparations in every classroom nowadays.

If I were but a fairy small
I'd search the whole world through
And find up all the Christmas joys
And send them straight to you.

Won't you come and have a ride?
See how fast we go
The best of fun is Christmas fun
Especially in the snow.

Why the Robin's breast is red

The robin often appears on Christmas cards, amidst a snowy scene, or carrying the Christmas cards in his beak. His red breast makes him seem bright and cheerful, yet many myths from around the world explain the dangers this tiny bird suffered in becoming such a colourful fellow.

In Brittany children are told that the robin followed Jesus carrying his Cross along the stony way that led to Calvary. He remembered how the boy Jesus had thrown him crumbs from his doorstep in Nazareth, and wanted to repay him in some way. As Jesus hung on the Cross the timid bird fluttered around the Crown of Thorns. With his tiny wings he wiped away the tears from the cheeks of Jesus, and with his tiny beak he tried to pluck out the thorns which pressed into the Saviour's forehead. As he did so, drops of crimson blood stained the feathers of his breast. They are still red today.

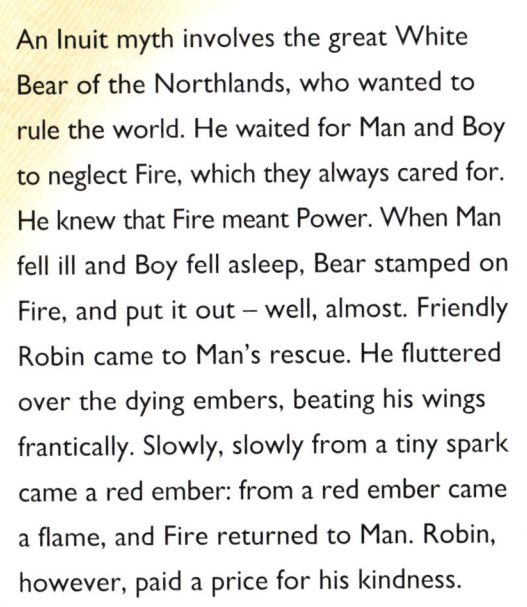

An Inuit myth involves the great White Bear of the Northlands, who wanted to rule the world. He waited for Man and Boy to neglect Fire, which they always cared for. He knew that Fire meant Power. When Man fell ill and Boy fell asleep, Bear stamped on Fire, and put it out – well, almost. Friendly Robin came to Man's rescue. He fluttered over the dying embers, beating his wings frantically. Slowly, slowly from a tiny spark came a red ember: from a red ember came a flame, and Fire returned to Man. Robin, however, paid a price for his kindness. His fine brown feathers were scorched for ever.

The Welsh legend begins with a boy who is caught throwing pebbles at a robin sitting on the handle of a garden spade.

The boy's grandmother scolds him, saying, *Bachgen drwg!* Naughty boy! Haven't you seen his red breast? Those are marks from the flames of hell which have singed his feathers. He is the kindest of birds. He sips the morning dew in his beak, flies deep through the caves of darkness, and shakes the cool drops of water on the brows of all the sinners down in torment.

Never throw a stone at a robin – one day in the future you just might be grateful to him!'

The Nativity

Come and see the baby,
cradled in the hay,
Come and see the Christ-child,
born on Christmas Day.

Come and see the shepherds,
in the fields at night,
Come and see the angels,
clothed in golden light.

Come and see the Wise men,
guided by the star,
Come and see the presents,
gifts from lands afar.

Come and see God's creatures,
in the stable bare,
Come and see Lord Jesus,
he is waiting there.

At the heart of Christmas is the Christmas story of the birth of Jesus in a stable in Bethlehem. It is celebrated in churches, homes and schools throughout the world. Nativity plays are a part of every child's Christmas in schools or Sunday Schools across Wales.

Traditional carols, like 'Away in A Manger' and 'Once in Royal David's City' have been joined by Christmas songs such as 'Mary had a Baby', 'Little Donkey', and 'Come and see the baby'.

Christmas crib scenes, first made popular by Saint Francis of Assisi, hundreds of years ago in Italy, can still be seen lighting up the shadows at the back of churches, or brightening the entrance halls of school buildings. Originally they included live animals and wax dolls. Nowadays figures are made in many materials: straw, plastic, fibreglass – even scrap materials and kitchen rolls! Whatever they look like, they are a reminder of that first Christmas, over 2000 years ago in Bethlehem.

Some Christmas cards used nativity designs. This 3-D card is a very old one, made by Raphael Tuck & Sons, publishers to her Majesty the Queen (Victoria).

> A stable serves Him for a dwelling.
> And for a bed a manger mean;
> Yet o'er his Head, His Advent telling,
> A new and wondrous star is seen.

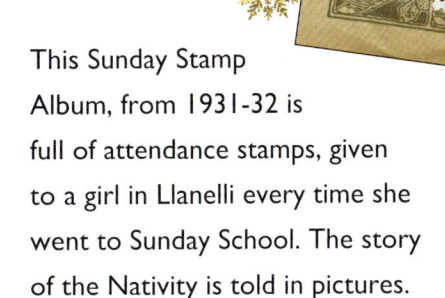

This Sunday Stamp Album, from 1931-32 is full of attendance stamps, given to a girl in Llanelli every time she went to Sunday School. The story of the Nativity is told in pictures.

"In my early years I often went across the yard in the winter with the little hurricane lamp to the stable. Sitting on my 3-legged stool I felt very much at home watching the horses bedded down for the night in clean straw, eating their hay, moving patiently backwards and forwards on the tethered rope anchored by a weight at the end, as it slid up and down through the ring below the manger . . . Here somehow it was easy to see that other Manger . . . I like to think that Mary felt safe and secure here too."

Jo Howells, recalling Christmas in a Vale of Glamorgan farmhouse in the 1920s

9

Treacle Toffee: Cyflaith

1lb (450g) Demerara sugar
¼ pint water
4oz (125g) butter
¼ teaspoon cream of tartar
3 tablespoons black treacle
3 tablespoons golden syrup
2 drops vinegar

Dissolve the sugar in the water. Add the butter, cream of tartar, treacle and syrup. Add 2 drops of vinegar. Bring to the boil and heat to 131°C (270°F). Do not stir. Turn into a buttered tin. After 5 minutes cut into squares. Leave to set.

Plygain

The first church service of Christmas, the *plygain*, was a very important part of Christmas in Wales in years gone by. It was usually held early on Christmas morning, sometimes as early as 3 a.m!, so young people often didn't bother going to bed the night before. They would all meet in someone's farmhouse kitchen and make treacle toffee (called *cyflaith* in Welsh) and decorate the house with holly and greenery. In some villages boys ran through the streets carrying flaming torches, and blowing cowhorns as they walked with the vicar from his house to the church, probably with their mouths full of toffee!

People from all around the district made their way to the parish church carrying specially made candles, with large wicks, which wouldn't blow out on a stormy morning. The churches would be brightly lit by these hundreds of candles, sometimes fixed in chandeliers or onto the tops of the pews. Although they now have electricity, of course, many churches still have candlelit carol services, especially at Midnight Mass on Christmas Eve. In many parts of mid-Wales the traditions of the *plygain*, the cock's crow service, still continue – some at 3.00 a.m. and some a little later.

The carols themselves were the most important part of the service, many of them newly composed each year by local poets and ballad singers. One *plygain* service was said to have included 30 carols, some with as many as 12 verses; not so much a marathon as a carolothon! *Plygain* carols are still being written, and are included in modern hymn books.

An old school log book of 1909 shows how the use of recipes and baking in school could be put to good use.

If you can't make out the handwriting, this is what it says:

"Lessons are given this week on the ingredients used in the making of the Christmas Pudding and cake. Several parents have sent contributions of Fruit, Sugar etc, and these were made into the cake before the children. This afternoon at 3 o'clock the teachers will give the children Tea, and incidentally a lesson on tea-table manners."

In the world of make-believe, other creatures may well have had their own Christmas recipes to attend to:

STIRRING THE PUDDING
The Little Robins Make Their Christmas Wishes

FROM most of the little kitchens all over the woodlands there came a delicious smell of cooking. The woodfolk were busy cooking their Christmas puddings.

Roley, Rosemary, and their little cousin Richard were hurrying home from school and sniffing happily as they trotted along.

"You had better come and stir *our* Christmas pudding before you go home and stir yours," said Rosemary to Richard. "You may be luckier in getting what you want most of all, if you wish twice."

So Richard followed his cousins into Mrs. Robin's kitchen, and while Rosemary stirred the pudding three times round and wished hard, he took a slip of paper out of his pocket. On the paper was a list of things Richard was WISHING for. Instead of wishing twice for the same thing, it would be a good idea to stir one of his wishes into Mrs. Robin's pudding and another into his mother's, thought Richard. There were so many things he wanted "most of all."

Richard took a piece of paper out of his pocket.

Cwrw Bach: Small Beer

(Such home-brew may well have been served after the plygain service, as part of the Christmas breakfast, when neighbours gathered to discuss the newly performed carols, and the quality of the singing: strong ale for the adults, small beer for the children!)

Boil together for half an hour 10 pints of water, 3 doz dandelions, 3 doz nettles, 6 sticks ginger pounded (beaten), 3 sticks rhubarb, some currant tops, 2 large handfuls hops.

Strain and add 1lb Demerara sugar; stir, add 6 pints cold water; when lukewarm sprinkle over surface 1oz yeast.

Leave overnight, skim and bottle.

Country people add a sprig of wormwood, which is considered to be a good tonic.

Father Christmas
and presents

Father Christmas, who first brought gifts on horseback (the reindeer sleigh was a later American addition) was, and still is the most popular Christmas visitor for children. In the past he placed simple gifts in a stocking at the end of the bed – 'an apple, an orange, and a couple of nuts . . . and the orange was always sour'. Now he needs a container lorry to carry enough presents to fit in to the pillowcases and plastic sacks at the bottom of the stairs.

Every Christmas has its popular toy: Action Man, Barbie, the Care Bears, Teletubbies, the Tweenies – even Monopoly and Cluedo. For the two children in the photograph, a Dansette record player and a couple of singles to play over and over made the ideal Christmas present in the 1950s.

❝ I remember Christmas 1923 . . . As regards presents, one in particular I remember – a smoker's outfit, this was a special box, it was a fat cigar with a gold band, chocolate covered, and inside was a sort of banana flavoured fudge, a box of edible matches, cigarettes made of

Kim and Trevor proudly display their pony and trap, a very grand present for the year 1901.

chocolate, a Spanish (liquorice) pipe, the bowl was lit up with little red sweets . . ."

" . . . I found Christmas Eve to be the hardest part of all . . . how to try and sleep out the unbearable hours 'til morning, tantalising myself as to whether there would perhaps be some little extra in the stocking. The orange, the apple, the little bag of nuts and the book of 'Old Testament Stories' would be there for certain – and one memorable year, a bone china dolls' tea service, complete and new, a treasure I have kept to this day . . ."

Jo Howells

A visit to Santa's grotto, in a department store or even a corner of the school hall, is usually an enjoyable experience – but sometimes results in tears! Santa's costume and appearance seem to change from place to place . . . How could he be in so many towns and villages at the same time?

Hand-coloured photographs of real children were sometimes inserted into pre-printed Christmas scenes, like the one below. Perhaps your School Christmas photographs have a 'fake' background as well.

Santa's Lament

Why can't I have an aeroplane
Instead of this stupid sleigh
I could drop the presents with parachutes on,
And float them on their way.

A racing yacht with billowing sails
And a radar to steer her by,
A monster truck with ENORMOUS tyres,
To burn across the sky.

I'm fed up with stupid reindeer,
I'll have a motorbike instead,
With a rucksack for the presents,
And a helmet on my head.

I want to join the modern world,
I'm feeling such a fool,
No longer boring Santa,
I'm desperate to be cool!

Francesca Kay

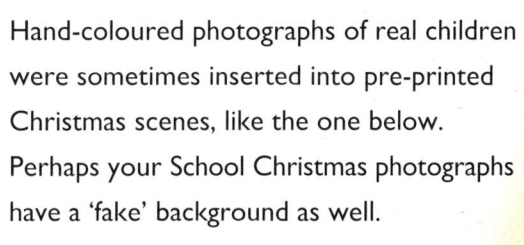

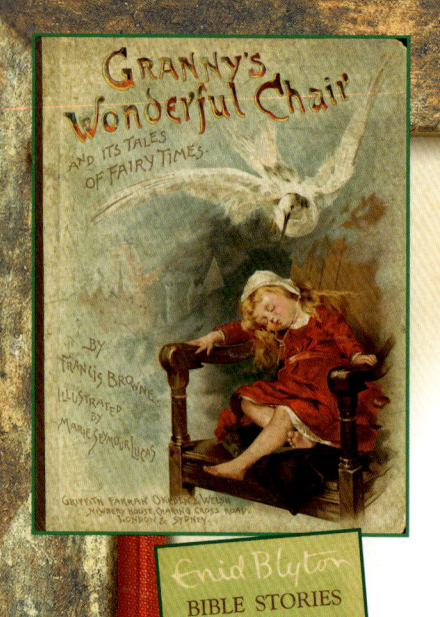

Christmas Books

Books have always been good presents. Many Annuals and other story books are published every year just in time for Christmas.

Magazines have special editions for Christmas, which make good stocking fillers. To get ideas for presents and sometimes 'factual' information, special Christmas issues are good to read before Christmas. But did children ever walk down the street with a goose wrapped in Christmas paper?

Perhaps the most famous Christmas book of all connected to Wales is the one containing the childhood recollections of the poet Dylan Thomas. Entitled *A Child's Christmas in Wales* it is set in a time and place where it always seemed to snow at the right time, where presents were either useful or useless, and where there were always uncles in the front parlour and aunties scuttling to and fro. The edition of the book illustrated by Edward Ardizzone is the most famous one; it has been translated into many languages, including Welsh, of course. It has also been made into a play, and a television film, which you can watch nearly every Christmas on one channel or another!

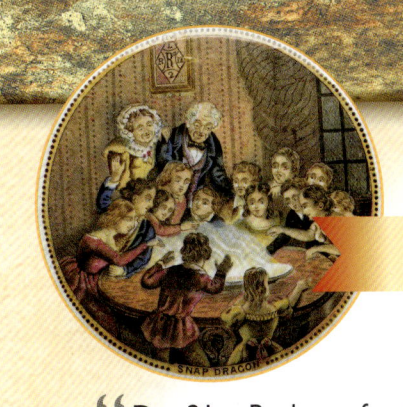

Parties

'Oranges and Lemons', on a 1940s card.

"Dec 21st: Broke up for the Xmas holidays. We return on 8th of January. Allowed the children to have a few games the latter part of the afternoon, and gave them an orange each."

Haverfordwest National School Log Book, 1876

Games have always been vital to a good party, even in Victorian times. One dangerous game, Shoeing the Mare, involved swinging from a rope attached to the ceiling. Another Victorian game, Snapdragon, where children tried to pick raisins from a flaming bowl of punch, make Musical Chairs and Pass the Parcel seem very tame. A favourite game in Montgomeryshire and Carmarthenshire was rather like bobbing for apples. In this Christmas game, a revolving stick hung from the ceiling, with an apple on one end and a lighted candle at the other. The idea was to catch the apple in your mouth, and not the flame – but the players had their hands tied behind their backs, so it wasn't easy!

Sometimes, parties were too formal to be fun . . .

". . . Each year, early in the Christmas break, the landlord (the Mackintosh of Mackintosh to give him his full title) gave a party for the children of the school. We were not asked if we would like to go, it was more or less a command and so on the appointed day, in the bitter chill, often in the driving sleet and snow we walked first to the school (nearly 3 miles distant) where we were regimentally assembled in the playground. The boys were drilled with the doffing of caps and saying 'Yes Sir' or 'Thank you, Ma'am', while the girls practised curtseys to coincide with the thanks . . . In the tack room at the Mansion house the long tables were laid for tea. There was jelly and blancmange, small cakes with pink icing on top and slabs of seed cake, a rather vicious yellow-colour, and plates of bread and butter. The menu never varied. Everything was so cold. At the far end of the room stood an enormous Christmas tree . . ."

Jo Howells

A Christmas tea-party in a 1958 classroom.

Evergreens

The holly King
With his Merry Men
Sings and dances
At Christmas again.

The Ivy Queen
With her maidens weeps
And friendship with the owl
She keeps.

Let holly be master
A man of red cheer,
Let ivy's black berries
Be gone now from here!

Most people enjoy bringing evergreens into their homes in time for Christmas. Today the Christmas tree is the most popular decoration, but it is quite a recent tradition in Britain. Queen Victoria and her German husband, Prince Albert, brought one to Balmoral Castle in 1840 and started a fashion. For hundreds of years before Christ's birth people used other evergreens to decorate their homes in the darkest 'dead' months of winter, and remind themselves that life remains in those trees which are forever-green.

Three plants which fruit at Christmastime – the mistletoe, the holly and the ivy – are at the heart of many Christmas traditions. In Wales houses were decorated with holly and mistletoe while people waited for the Plygain service. In Dolgellau church in the 1890s, the chandeliers were decorated with holly and candles. A rather nasty tradition of 'holly beating' used to take place on St Stephen's Day (Dec. 26th) when boys and young men with bundles of holly twigs ran after girl servants, whacking them until their arms bled!

The mistletoe, which needs a tree on which to grow, is known in Wales as 'sap of the oak', or 'Druid's Weed' and this links it closely with the oak tree which the Druids worshipped. Today, you can claim a Christmas kiss from anyone standing under a sprig of mistletoe.

Many carols refer to the importance of the holly, with its red berries and spiky leaves, said to represent the spiked crown of the Crucifixion, and the ivy, which represents Mary, the mother of the baby Jesus. Indeed some old songs talk about the Holly King and the Ivy Queen in competition with each other; the holly is always male, and the ivy female. It is strange that Holly is nowadays always used as a girl's name !

These boys you see so full of glee
Have got a famous Christmas tree.

Heron Cat and Bramble

An old Welsh folktale, retold by Daniel Morden

Heron, Cat and Bramble were good friends. They worked together to find treasure. One crisp December morning, Heron flew up high, high until he could see all the mountains covered in snow. Heron saw something shiny. He called Cat and Bramble.

Cat and Bramble followed Heron. Cat was jumping from frosty rock to frosty rock. Bramble was slithering through the crevices. They found what Heron had seen. Golden coins! They were so happy, as they shared the gold between them. Christmas, it seemed, had come early for the three good friends.

Heron put his coins in a bag, which he held in his beak. Cat put hers in a bag, which she held between her teeth. Bramble put his in a bag, which he held with his thorns.

When Heron was flying over a river he saw his own reflection. He thought it was his brother.

He shouted, 'Look what I've got!'

But when he opened his beak he dropped the sack and all the gold fell in a glittering shower into the river.

Cat got tired. She said to Mouse, 'Will you look after this bag while I sleep?' Mouse said, 'Yes, of course!'

When Cat woke up, Mouse had gone. He'd run down a hole with the gold.

Bramble was wriggling along a frosted hedgerow when a man grabbed his bag of gold and ran away.

Ever since that winter's day, Heron stands by the water, peering in, looking for his gold. Cat sits by mouse holes, waiting for Mouse to come out. Bramble grabs and tears at the clothes and skin of passers-by, hoping to catch the thief who stole the gold from him. Each one is dreaming of a richer Christmas for himself and his good friends.

Unpacking the Angel

Unpack the box and dress the tree
in glitter, glass and frippery,
fairy lights and silver strings.
You unpack almost everything,
then last of all, beneath the baubles,
at the bottom of the box, the Angel
in a nest of Christmas litter,
smoothed out wrapping paper, glitter,
and umpteen years of fir tree bristles.
Listen! her paper feathers rustle,
the tissue chrysalis unfolds,
her crumpled robe, her wings of gold,
a crackle of lightning from her hair,
and a small shout: 'Excelsior.'

Gillian Clarke

Pantomime

A visit to the pantomime has always been an eagerly awaited treat at Christmas, and the major theatres in Wales are still famous for the thrills and excitement of their productions.

Nowadays pantomimes in Britain are filled with pop groups and soap stars, and there is often little left of the original stories, but this was not always the case. The first pantomimes (the word means *all mime*) featured French actors representing Harlequin, Columbine and Scaramouch, with performing dogs. Then there were clowns like the Grimaldis who used their slapsticks for hitting other characters. In the 19th century stories like Cinderella and Aladdin found their way into the pantomimes, along with other favourites such as Jack and the Beanstalk and Dick Whittington. These remain crowd-pullers today. Babes in the Wood and Robin Hood are considered unlucky, and seldom performed.

The musical play Peter Pan is another favourite Christmas entertainment, full of excitement and spectacle, goodies and baddies. The fairy Tinkerbell, and Captain Hook continue to vie for the support of young audiences, and Peter Pan's flying never fails to bring gasps of amazement.

One of the oddest traditions of pantomime in Britain is that a man, a famous comedian, usually plays the dame (who is either the hero's mother, or nursemaid) dressed in extravagant costumes and hats which make fun of the fashion of the day. She behaves more like a man than a woman, and we all share the joke of 'Oh, yes he is; oh, no he isn't!' A glamorous girl often plays the handsome hero, usually in fishnet tights and thigh boots, although ideas change, and there was a time when men took over this role. Cliff Richard for one, has been a principal boy and so has Norman Wisdom.

" . . . the best pantomimes were at the old Empire Theatre (in Swansea) . . . Harry Secombe was in it one year . . . at the end he was the 'Queen of Sketty' . . . in his ermine robes, with a crown . . ."

" we went with the Scouts to see Terry Scott as Widow Twankey . . . in Cardiff or Swansea it was . . . and Barbara Windsor was Aladdin . . everybody had their opera glasses fixed on her!"

Besides the main cast of stars, most pantomimes have a chorus line and dancers. A group of children from a local dance school often appear in routines with the stars, and are always known as 'The Babes'.

" . . . it was easy for us, we'd learnt the steps months before . . . but the stars had to learn them in two weeks . . . and all the lines! . . . They treated us all as equals, and were really friendly."
Bethany and Emma, two of the Grand Theatre Dance School 'Babes', who appeared in Snow White, 1990.

The Wren

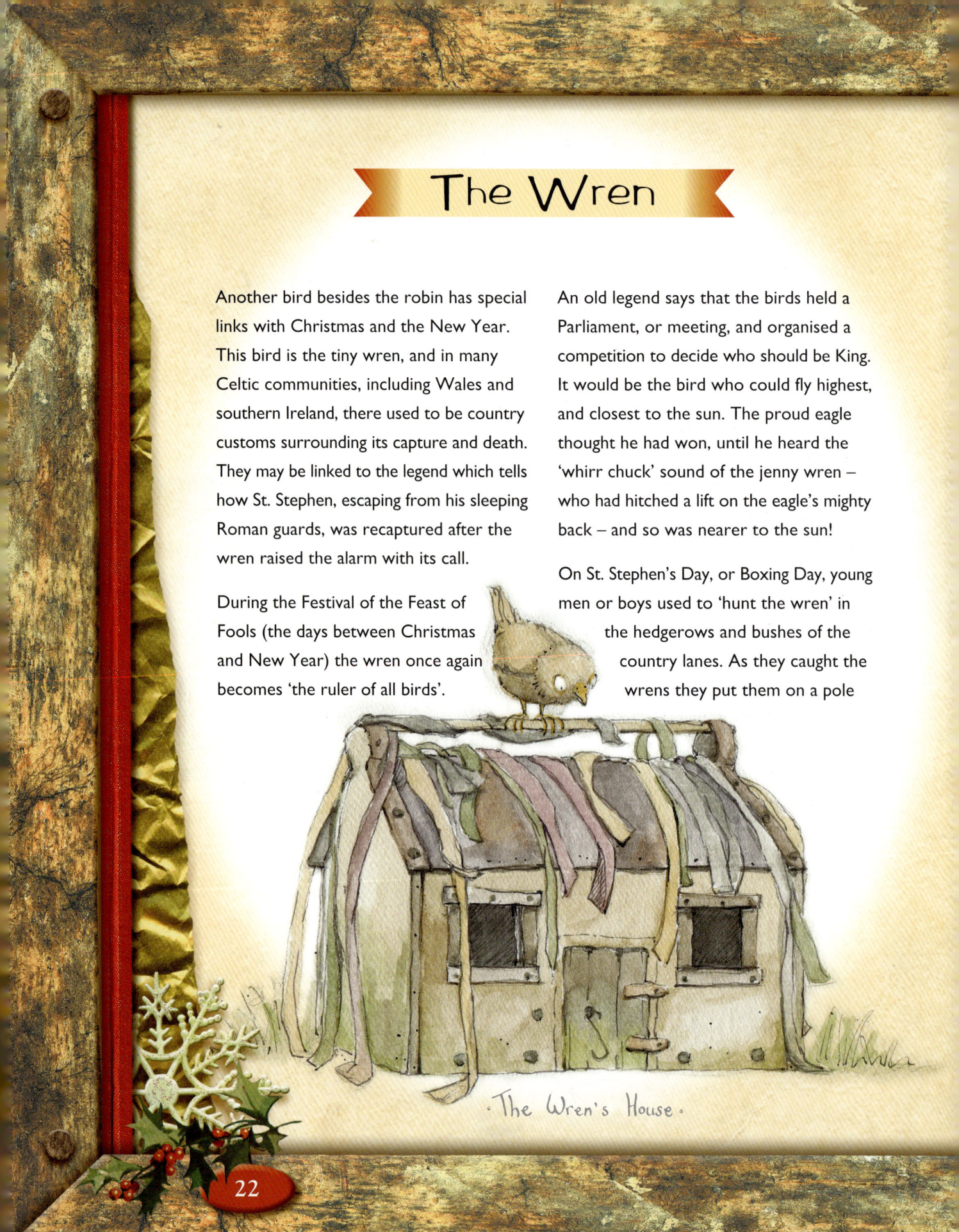

Another bird besides the robin has special links with Christmas and the New Year. This bird is the tiny wren, and in many Celtic communities, including Wales and southern Ireland, there used to be country customs surrounding its capture and death. They may be linked to the legend which tells how St. Stephen, escaping from his sleeping Roman guards, was recaptured after the wren raised the alarm with its call.

During the Festival of the Feast of Fools (the days between Christmas and New Year) the wren once again becomes 'the ruler of all birds'.

An old legend says that the birds held a Parliament, or meeting, and organised a competition to decide who should be King. It would be the bird who could fly highest, and closest to the sun. The proud eagle thought he had won, until he heard the 'whirr chuck' sound of the jenny wren – who had hitched a lift on the eagle's mighty back – and so was nearer to the sun!

On St. Stephen's Day, or Boxing Day, young men or boys used to 'hunt the wren' in the hedgerows and bushes of the country lanes. As they caught the wrens they put them on a pole

The Wren's House.

decorated with holly leaves and carried them through the streets, often singing songs as they went.

Then on Twelfth Night, four strong youths would carry one of these imprisoned wrens from farm to farm, in a specially-made bird box or Wren house. You can see one of these, made in Marloes, in Pembrokeshire, in 1869 at the Museum of Welsh Life at St. Fagan's. Often the houses, with glass windows and a hinged front door, were decorated with ribbons or leather strips. The men would pretend the bird and the bier (or coffin) were as heavy as the world. They used to moan and groan under its weight, singing a carol, begging for money and beer.

Often they visited the farmhouses of the men's sweethearts, or even the homes of newly married couples. Even now, in some areas of Pembrokeshire, people who have been married in the previous year are expected to 'keep open house' on New Year's Eve, and can expect a late-night visit by the Young Farmers' Club.

Wren-Song

We bring peace and health
  As we rest here and sing
    With a promise of wealth
      From our fine feathered King.

he's the true Cutty Wren
  With his ribbons so rare
    Who's been caught once again
      So no others compare.

We have walked many miles
  Before reaching your gate,
    Climbing hedges and stiles
      With the coffin's great weight.

We ask for no more
  Than a half-a-crown's cheer
    Crossing your doorstep
      For a flagon of beer.

Then Good-bye to the Old Year
  We'll welcome the New
    As we pick up our Wren King
      And bid you adieu!

Wassailing

Singing of carols, and drinking of wine and ale were, and still are, one of the favourite Christmas pastimes. Wassailers were like carol singers, going from house to house, singing songs, wishing people 'a Merry Christmas and a Happy New Year', and hoping for a gift of either money or food and drink.

People in different parts of Wales sang different words to their wassail songs, but they all wished people a happy life in the year ahead. The Gower wassail song overleaf promises that the singers will return the following Christmastide – all being well.

The wassailers often carried with them a wassail bowl, a kind of pottery casserole with twelve handles (perhaps to represent the 12 days of Christmas, or the 12 disciples). The wassail bowl was decorated with pictures and models of birds, berries and oak leaves and contained cake and baked-apple soaked in beer and spices from the East. This was passed around the group, who ate the cake when the drink was finished. Some very old wassail cups made of Ewenny ware can be seen in the Museum of Welsh Life. Some were probably dropped and their handles smashed by the drunken revellers!

· Wassail Bowl ·

Wassail, wassail, to our town—

People working at the Gwili Pottery, near Carmarthen, have brought back the tradition of making wassail bowls, by designing and making one specially for this Christmas book. The decorator has even included a wren, to remind us of the old tradition of 'hunting the wren'. She used as a model a wren which had built its nest in the ivy outside the studio window.

25

Gower Wassail

The wassail, the wassail throughout all the town
Our cup it is white and our ale it is brown
Our wassail is made of the good ale and cake
Some nutmeg and ginger the best we could make.

   Fal-de-dol dol-de-dol-de dol, dol-de-dol-de dol,
   Dol-de-dol-de dol,
   O sing tu-ra-liy tu-ral, sing tu-ra-liy-ey.

We know by the moon that we are not too soon,
And we know by the sky that we are not too high.
We know by the stars that we are not too far,
And we know by the ground that we are within sound.

   Fal-de-dol dol-de-dol-de dol, . . .

Now master and mistress to you thanks we'll give
For our jolly wassail as long as we live,
And if we should live for another full year
Perhaps we may come and see who do live here.

   Fal-de-dol dol-de-dol-de dol, . . .

Calennig

New Year's morning used to be a great time for children, and in many rural parts of Wales children still go in search of *calennig*. They go around the village, singing a song or carol at every house, then knocking on the door to collect a New Year's gift: *calennig*. In the past children carried with them a kind of 'christingle', which was an apple studded with evergreens, raisins and corn, possibly to represent the fruits and growth of the coming year. Sometimes children carried a bag for the gifts they hoped to receive: coins, oranges and sweets. Although the decorated fruit has been forgotten, everyone still knows that the singing must take place in the morning: after 12 o'clock the gift-giving stops.

"At New Year we went out singing . . . you had to get up early and finish singing by 12, that was the law . . . the shops in Narberth were waiting for the kids to come to give us sweets or an orange.."
Glenys Adams, Llawhaden

. . . an apple stuck full of corn, variously coloured and decorated with a sprig of some evergreen, three short skewers serve as supports to the apple when not held in the hand, and a fourth serves to hold it without destroying its many coloured honours . . . (1819)

Only a few very elderly people remember another object carried round from cottage to cottage in some areas of Carmarthenshire at New Year. This was the *perllan* or orchard, a sort of miniature garden on a piece of rectangular board, with a rosy apple at each corner and sticks of holly or other wood pointing into the centre, where a bunch of twigs, representing a tree, held a miniature bird. Sometimes this bird was a wren, so perhaps the custom is linked to the hunting of the wren.

In Liz Haigh's story *The Dragon Ring*, the young heroine, Sara finds herself transported back to a Victorian house on New Year's morning . . .

She opened the front door to see a group of boys standing there grinning at them. One of them, Sara couldn't imagine why, was holding a large apple with little sticks pushed into it. As she stared at it, the boys began to sing :

Blwyddyn Newydd Dda i chi,
Ac i bawb sydd yn y tŷ.

Sara knew a few songs in Welsh, but not this one. She found she could understand the words, though:

Happy New Year to you,
And to everyone in the house.

The woman was smiling, as the boys sang another song. Then she reached into her apron pocket. 'Here's your calennig. One penny for each of you.'

Mari Lwyd

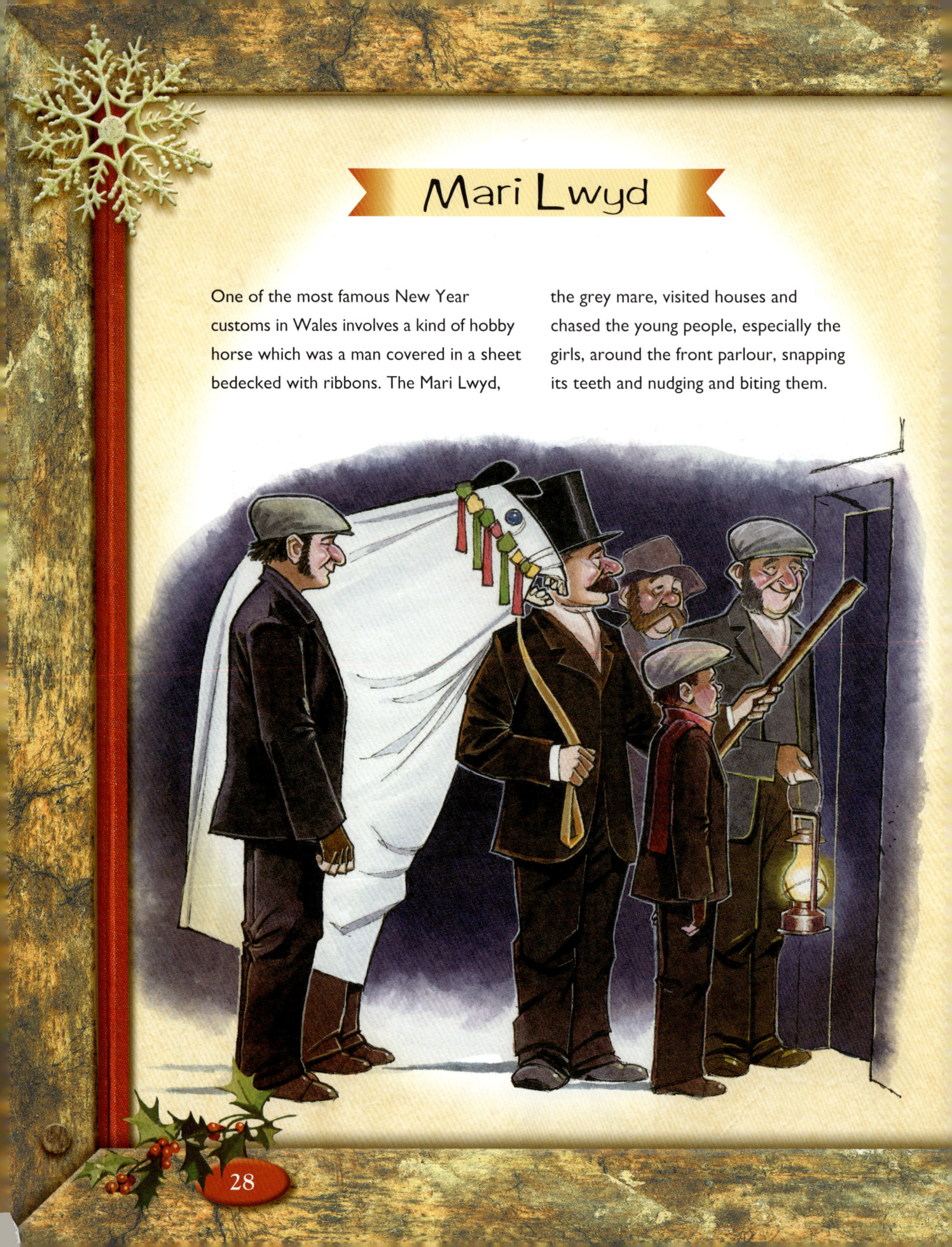

One of the most famous New Year customs in Wales involves a kind of hobby horse which was a man covered in a sheet bedecked with ribbons. The Mari Lwyd, the grey mare, visited houses and chased the young people, especially the girls, around the front parlour, snapping its teeth and nudging and biting them.

It is said that sometimes the horse and its antics were so fearsome that women were literally frightened to death. This happened in Pembrokeshire once when the horse-monster, Cynfas-farch, made from a canvas sheet stuffed with straw, poked its head through an upstairs window!

The Mari Lwyd itself was usually made from a horse's skull, which was buried and dug up each year for the festivities.

> She's a frisky, comely mare
> With knotted ribbons for her hair;
> Thousands praise her, can't you hear
> her good luck tonic for next year.
>
> The ostler leads this handsome beast
> Proudly now to join your feast.
> With saddle and bridle both in place
> She'll roam and gallop round this space.

The head, which was fitted with glinting eyes made from fragments of old bottle glass, was mounted on a pole, with a spring fixed to the lower jaw. The mouth snapped shut with a loud crack when pulled by the man working the Mari. He was hidden beneath a white sheet, which was decorated with brightly-coloured ribbons and reins with bells attached. The Mari Lwyd, or Aderyn Pica Llwyd (Grey Magpie in English) as it was sometimes called, was led through the village by a groom, and other 'Merrymen', including Punch and Judy!

At each house there would be a kind of singing-riddle competition, between the visitors and the householders, each group trying to out-sing the other. At last the Horse and attendants would be allowed to enter the house, still singing verses, demanding something to eat, and wishing the household a Happy New Year.

Sometimes this custom became muddled up with another, such as the wassailing or hunting the wren. In Ireland, for example, the 'wren boys' also carried round a *láir bhán* or White Mare, which was similar to the Mari Lwyd. Whatever happened, the visits always ended with food and drink!

New Year Calendar

One end-of-Christmas custom – the 'New Year's Water' – seems to have died out, or dried up, completely. Boys in South Wales, and in Pembrokeshire in particular, used to rush round the houses with a bucket of fresh spring water hidden behind their backs, sprinkling it on everyone they met, including people still in bed. This is the song they sang:

> Sing reign of fair maid,
>   with gold upon her chin,
> Open you the east door,
>   and let the new year in.

People who are superstitious still worry about the 'first footer', the first person to step over the doorway, after midnight on New Year's Eve: it must be a man, and he must have dark hair, and he should be carrying a piece of coal. In Carmarthenshire his name should start with a lucky letter H, J or R (for Happiness, Riches and Joy). If your name starts with T, W or S it's better to stay away, for they stand for Trouble, Worry and Sorrow in the year to come.

People still send New Year Cards, as they have done for over a hundred years, and these were especially popular at the start of the new Millennium, which everyone was happy to celebrate.

Some people, especially in the Gwaun Valley, near Fishguard, still celebrate the Old New Year's Day, Hen Galan, which is actually on January 13th.

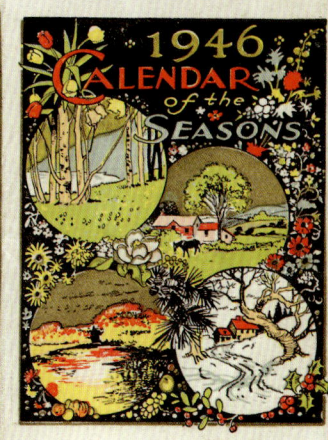

"My grandmother in the Gwaun valley used to make up poems... she was from a family of poets in Cardiganshire. This one was sung to the tune of 'Clementine':

> Dewch i'r Cwm ar nos Hen Galan,
> Bydd yr ardal holl yn fyw,
> Chi gewch groeso ar bob aelwyd
> Gyda glased o 'home brew'.
>
> Come to the Gwaun on New Year's night
> There's a welcome just for you,
> As they valley comes to life again
> Raise your glasses of 'home-brew'."

Ionwy Thorne

Calendars were also sent at Christmastime. They might in the past have been colourful, with verses included; they might now be just like plastic credit cards, to slip into your purse or wallet. In whatever form they came, they made it clear that celebrations were over, and a whole year lay ahead – from January to December. It would be a long time before anyone received another Christmas Box!

Calendar of Seasons 1946

The trees are bare, the skies are grey
In JANUARY every day;
It rains, it blows, it's frosty too,
Be glad when FEBRUARY's through!
In MARCH it may be windy, still,
You feel that Spring's just over the hill,
APRIL, and MAY bring back the smile
To Earth, and waiting's been worthwhile.
JUNE brings her roses. In JULY
The gardens glow 'neath Summer's sky;
AUGUST is red – SEPTEMBER gold
OCTOBER's here, the year grows old.
NOVEMBER's days are chill and drear,
Then white DECEMBER ends the year.

A Christmas box

© narrative and this selection: Chris S. Stephens
© extracts and illustrations: the authors and illustrators as noted
Designed by: Olwen Fowler
First publication 2001
Second edition 2001
ISBN 1 84323 037 2

All rights reserved. No part of this book may be reproduced, stored in a retrieval system, or transmitted in any form or by any means, electronic, electrostatic, magnetic tape, mechanical, photocopying, recording, or otherwise, without permission in writing from the publishers, Pont Books, Gomer Press, Llandysul, Ceredigion, Wales.

Printed in Wales at Gomer Press, Llandysul, Ceredigion SA44 4QL

Original illustrations
Endpapers and holly motif: Elizabeth Dyer
Christmas boxes (p. 5): Edmund Stephens
Robin (p. 9) and Angel (p. 27): Suzanne Carpenter
Heron, Cat and Bramble (p. 18): Jac Jones
The Wren's House (p. 22) and Wassail Bowl (p. 24): Fran Evans
Carrying the Wren's House (p. 23): Hywel Livingstone
Mari Lwyd (p. 28): Graham Howells

Back cover photographs
Mrs Jo Howells; Rebecca, Robert and Katie Adams

Acknowledgements
The author and publishers gratefully acknowledge the generosity of the following, who have loaned material or given permission for material to be reproduced in this book:
Olive Dyer for sharing her collection of Christmas Cards; The Wilson Museum, Narberth for New Year Cards; Wendy Dacre for the Gower Wassail Song; Robin Gwyndaf who collected 'Heron, Cat and Bramble' from Lewis T. Evans of Uwchaled; Haverfordwest VC School & Albion Square Infants School, Pembroke Dock, for archive material; The North Wales Theatre, Dafydd Hywel, The New Theatre Cardiff and the West Glamorgan Archive Service for pantomime programmes; *The Woman's Weekly* (Nov. 22, 1952) for extract on page 11; Frederick Warne & Co. for the work of Cicely Mary Barker on page 25.
(Copyright © The Estate of Cicely Mary Barker, 1928, 2001)
The author is indebted to Trefor Owen for the wealth of material available in *Welsh Folk Customs,* Gomer, 1959.
Tracing copyright-holders of illustrations has sometimes proved impossible.
Copyright-holders are invited to contact the publishers so that full acknowledgements can be made in any future editions.